Flowers Will Bloom

Sometimes, life is hard. Some days are Exceptionally worse than others, but in times like those it's important to remind yourself it's merely temporary. What once was merely dirt and rubble, will eventually blossom into beautiful blooms again. This is how I would describe these poems, and how I decided on the name. Life may be scary, or sad, or even just really horrible at times, but All of those times are just one in a million of the time you will see; Look for the blooming, not the Wilting.

Free
Go as far as the wind will take you
Don't slow down, put your arms out as far as they'll reach;
Close your eyes and mind, the wind will feel anew
If you truly believe, you could feel the sand on the beach
Freedom grazing through your hands
The cool breeze passing your lips
Gracefully you float around and dance
Feel your hair in between your fingertips
You feel as calm and collected as can be
No stress, no worry, just to exist peacefully
Your sorrowful eyes stare into the sea
But then the vision flickers miserably.
And there you are
Running, running, running
Dreading not having a car
Is this unbecoming?
Your heart beats through your chest thumping
Your breath races to keep up with your legs
You worry you're done for, your body's numbing
You can't stop moving, it isn't a test.
Race for the sea
Thats what you need, freedom
Its what will make you be
If you get caught, you'll make sure it's gruesome.

-Alex Yowler

I Give Up

The feeling surging through my veins
Is is anger, hurt, or just confusion?
I would learn to just shut up if I had any brains
But unfortunately the thoughts have too strong of an intrusion.
They said trust but they are lying through their teeth
Why do I even bother to try?
I'm tired of begging people to not leave
I'm tired of always trying not to cry
I'm exhausted of even talking
I don't want to eat.
You will see me going no where alone walking
I walk to the sound of the loud beat
All I have is music
The only thing that hasn't left or abandoned me
Who wouldn't choose it?
Music is only what it's supposed to be
I hear my name so often and none good
I don't even know how to exist in peace
If I knew how to stop already I would
But the intrusive voices refuse to cease.
Don't make food
Don't get that water
The voices are severely rude
The sting in my voice getting hotter
The lump in my throat builds like a boulder
I stay silent so I don't ruin it all
I don't have anyone's shoulder.
I don't have anyone I can call.
I guess I'm back to being alone

Everything falls apart at the end
Sorry if it sounds a little mad in my tone
I'm tired of even trying to mend.

-Alex Yowler

Flesh
There's no way to alter your flesh
You can reshape it, but not replace
Diet, Exercise, contort yourself to look better than the rest
Though with most it leaves quite an awful distaste
Warp, burn, cut and paste;
Some try everything in their power
Just to change their already perfect face
Because their reflection makes them cower
We see ourselves differently then we are
You can't see your own soul through the mirror
We act as if our bodies are drenched in thick tar
When in reality we merely glance at our exterior.

-Alex Yowler

Save Me
I'm trapped.
Stuck in a wolfs closing jaws
My whole life has been mapped
As I desperately try to avoid sharp claws
I wish & pray for some savior,
But no one even slightly looks
Can't someone do me this one favor?
I struggle holding the teeth in this tight nook.
Can't they see me crying?
Can't they hear me begging?
All I can think of and see is dying,
And it's the one thing I'm not dreading.
I can see the end
And I'm relieved yet terrified the same
My bones ready to all bend,
And no one after death will even say my true name.

-Alex Yowler

Toxic

I worry that I crave toxicity
But maybe, I just crave feeling special
The thought of you to someone lives eccentricity
The thought that they'll never make you tremble
I don't want harm,
I just want to feel important for once
Maybe a plus if they use some charm,
I've been trying to describe this for months
I was so worried that I was set for disappointment
So worried that Cupid must've hated me
Trying over and over again and over planning as if a date was an appointment,
But I guess my brain just won't leave me be
I just want to be good enough
I want for once to be the first choice
But I know im not perfectly smooth, im rough
Im not soft spoken, i have an obnoxious voice
I am not quiet and shy, I will lash out
If you push me I'll make you regret everything
I won't sit quietly with a pout
So unless you give me your all, don't ring.

-Alex Yowler

Do I Miss You?

I don't know whether I miss you,
Or if I just can't stand the fact you left so suddenly
I would've never said the words back if I knew
Now I stare at your name numbly
I want to text, want to call but I'm scared
I wish I could call out your name one last time
I feel so unprepared
For your response that'll leave a bitter taste in my throat like a lime
You seen that I would burn cities for you,
And instead you threw the matches at me
And I wonder If they knew
Or if they couldn't leave us be
Are you ashamed of my presence?
You didn't seem that way alone
You accept all my presents,
You happily kissed me in my home,
So what did I do?
Why was I now not enough?
I wish I knew what I did to you
I wish I knew if I loved too rough
Maybe my intensity scared you off
I got too attached so you ripped me away
I hold back tears with a horrible cough,
And I guess now I just go my own way.

-Alex Yowler

The Wolf

"I love you" the wolf said
He really loved the way you'd play dead

"I miss you" the wolf hissed
He really misses how you bent,
"I miss when we first kissed"
Really means I hated where you went

"We worked so well" the wolf purred
You stayed through all you deterred.

"I wish to hold you again," The wolf whispered quietly
I will scare you again triumphantly.

"I held you with so much care"
To leave me, I thought you'd never dare.

But this lamb got away.
And you will forever be held at bay

The road to freedom is still long,
But I know it isn't wrong.

Your fangs will never bite me anymore
After I walked out that door

Your nails will not hold me still,
Despite how you tried with all your will.

Your voice no longer is louder
For what I do, is in *my* power.

-Alex Yowler

Lemons

When life gives you lemons, You stomp them down.
Because it's not an orchid in which you can drown.

It's not a blueberry, small and sweet.

It's not an apple, so perfect and neat.

It's sour and uncertain

It doesn't appeal to your perversion.

It doesn't have vibrant colors like red or blue,

Yellow is beautiful, yet that you never knew.

You don't see it, do you?

The lemons were always true.

You chose to discard them though.

Yet melon you'd never throw.

The lemons you tossed,

Will only be the first not last of fruits you'll have lost.

-Alex Yowler

Hurt

You hurt me
But I won't let you know, so just let me be
I gave you my everything
But now you won't even say my name.
I've known you my whole life
But it feels like it's all been ruined in one night
It's hard to believe that it's been all these years
And every time I think of it I feel like I'm drowning in my own tears
Because I gave you my everything, my all,
But now I can't even get you to answer my call
And you won't even tell me what I did wrong
If I'd known you'd leave this easily, I wouldn't have stayed all this long.
But I've known you my whole life, but now you're being a stranger
If I was dying, would you even help me or put me in more danger?
I now know I never should've trusted you
But that's not a surprise to you, it's nothing new.
I've cried a river over you already,
But don't cry to me when you're hurt looking for a remedy
Cause I loved you
But I won't give you anymore, and I swear it's true.

-Alex Yowler

Decoration

Better off dead

Rather it than melting into my same old same bed

Loud Yelling in my mind

Slowly pricking and eating at my pride

When is the end

Is there any possible way to ever mend?

Rotting into mush and decompose

And better yet, no one even knows

My skin is flushed and pale as snow

It won't listen anyway, why bother say no?

Purple decoration feels pretty

It's under control, it's only mini

It's the end of the start

You have as much chance getting stuck just as throwing a dart.

Soon your skin is devoured

It's all okay, it just proves I'm not a coward.

Purple pretty spots

I press them as I feel the need to rot

Red tinted swells and burns

If you wanna try, we can even take turns

Soft slim rugged lines

We can battle our own minds.

The left over decorations on your smooth flesh

I promise it doesn't make you seem like a mess

They just show that your strong
And I know as fact I'm not wrong

-Alex Yowler

Another Chance

It wasn't her plan at any time
It felt like being charged with a false crime
She shouldn't be here
There's nothing left she holds dear
That night, she swallowed all them
Hiding in the room like a sad den
The pills were all gone
So how did it go wrong?
Why was she still alive?
Why didn't her body take the dive?
Life had given her a second chance
But she had no reason to celebrate and dance
She felt robbed of an escape
But now it's too late
She was almost found on the floor
With her little sister at the door.
Though life had nothing left for her to give,
For this child, she knew she had to live.

-Alex Yowler

The Bearing Fruit

In the height of the season fruit hangs low
The tree sharing its growth out,
And yet despite the fact you know
You turn your head away in a scowl similar to a pout
The tree drops its fruits soon, begging to be taken
But then you just scoff and kick and stomp
Maybe the tree was mistaken
But soon all its fruits had to drop
And only when the tree is cold and bare,
Only when it has nothing to give,
Is when you want it to share
When the tree can barely live.
You curse and sputter at the tree,
You kick and pull the leaves and roots,
And the tree can't fight, only see
As you smash its remnants under your boots.
The tree holding life as much as it could,
You pull out it's seeds,
If it had the choice, do you think it would?
You take and take everything the tree needs.
Because you were greedy and selfish,
When the season comes around once more,
It's already helpless
The tree has rotted and died, and its roots no longer sore.
-Alex Yowler

The Butterfly
The butterfly flies across my skin
Dancing along my vulnerability softly
The creature started very thin,
But it stops very shortly

Landing on my vein over my wrist
As it takes it's final breath,
I whisper that it will be missed,
And I will honor and love it even in death

I memorize it's lovely wings,
Before I bury him below the earth,
My eyes start to sting,
Because it will never know it's worth

My heart sings as I trace my wrist slowly,
Where I've memorized it's beauty
And came to me when I needed it mostly.
It has made me trace invisible scars soothingly.

I will continue to honor this tiny savior,
As I prick needles into my flesh,
It will all be worth it later
And it will always be in my head when I wake and rest

The ink covers the spot it had been when I was saved,
And it didn't even know
That a monster in me it had tamed,
Tenderness, is what it came to me to show

So now I will always have a piece of it with me
The drawing on my arm may not be real,
And many say I should've let it be,
But to me, this tattoo is a big deal.

-Alex Yowler

The Tide
The tide pulls me under,
though it has great beauty, I'm not full of wonder
It throws me away
Day after day
I'm trapped,
Has my fate been mapped?
Am I meant to succumb to the pain?
Was my fight all in vain?
I always end up back where I begun
I'm so tired of trying to run
I always start to drown
I'm always being held down
I'm tired of crying
I'm tired of almost dying.
Instead of fighting the unforgiving waves,
I ease and accept this as my days.
As I slowly sink underneath the surface,
I realize there's something I've missed
I start to float to the sky
I look around wondering why?
The water is now perfectly still
Now perfectly calm
Is it me or its own will?
My days no longer feel long
I now spend my days with ease
And don't worry or care who I please.

-Alex Yowler

<u>S.W.</u>
You say you aren't pretty
But you believe that you're witty

You think you look bad
And that is just sad

Because you aren't just the sky
But the stars and light
When the heavens cry,
It is because they can't stand all your might

The sun and moon fight over who could see your face,
The stars all fall into their place

Just to see *you.*
And this is something I wish you knew

If I were to sculpt you and form all the things you're insecure of,
You would finally see that they are just more willing for love.

If I could paint you with all the colors of your skin, your hair, your eyes,
You would see that your mind has filled you with lies.

I wish to capture just how I see you,
But I know you'll never have my view

So instead I'll focus on making your name stick to this world forever

So that you will die never

No one deserves to miss out on your perfection
No matter what the lesson

Aphrodite definitely favored you
And this, I'm well aware is true.

-Alex Yowler

Forgiving

I'm too forgiving too easily
Once they come back pleadingly,
I forgive. But I never forget
But I don't wish we never met
I forgive over and over many times
No mater how many times they gave me lies,
I give chance after chance,
And the evil like to prance
But I never forget, call me naive, call me dumb,
But I am not numb
I see straight through your facade
Yet you never know and think you have it made
I may be too forgiving and smile,
But I see straight through you for a while
I gather my points and make a list
And once I cut you off, you'll never be missed
For I have a strong heart,
But stronger rage
And I won't hesitate to tear you apart
And then we'll be on the same page.

-Alex Yowler

Stubborn Plant
I thought I had died long ago
When the winds would harshly blow
This body was stuck and withered
But it's not as how you've pictured
My petals wilted, core rotted, and stem lay limp over
There was no sun as I had clouds to cover
No rain
Only pain
I thought I had died years ago, and would be this way until my body finally gave in
But then who would win?
I'm standing upright now here,
I may not be full of cheer,
But I'm alive.
Alive and full of strive
I've lost a few petals here and there,
But when I can feel the breeze, how could I care?
I thought I was dead,
And I was, everyone said
But I was saved by the sweet honeybees
All my friends, no matter the tease
But the one butterfly came to me first
When I was dying of thirst
He brought me water
He chased the clouds away
And brought out the sun
Just for me.
-Alex Yowler

Begging for Love
I file my sharp edges down to dust,
And I soften my skin
Will you love me, or only lust?
Will I finally be able to win?
If I bleach my teeth, perfect my lips,
Tan my skin, and pluck every hair
Then will you give me a kiss?
Or will you see me as a bear?
If I paint my face with every powder and brush,
And use all sorts of things in my hair,
Will it give you a rush?
Would you even care?
Finally you see this perfect beauty
And you come close to me
I will love you long and truly
Yours, I will be
But once you're in my arms,
You are repulsed and frightened
You revoke your words of charms
My desperate grip on you tightens
I try to keep you from leaving,
Holding you and begging,
It is then I realize my hold on you is bleeding
My grip loosens, but your fear isn't letting
For all this work to make myself perfect
Cannot fix what I am truly inside
I am ugly, vile, gruesome, and disgusting
I know you won't want me as your wife,
But could you please at least give me a chance in your life?

This is the end of my second book of poetry. I would like to thank people in my life for supporting me and my books; My father, My aunt Jen, (who helped me find publishers), My oldest cousin, Sky, and Jayce. Thank you guys for always having my back and supporting me in all I do♥

www.ingramcontent.com/pod-product-compliance
Lightning Source LLC
Chambersburg PA
CBHW070946220526
45469CB00007B/2536